POEM RISING OUT OF THE EARTH AND STANDING UP IN SOMEONE

AF328004

0054952227

Poem Rising Out Of The Earth And Standing Up In Someone

Poems

James Grabill

Lynx House Press
Portland, Oregon/Amherst, Massachusetts

ACKNOWLEDGEMENTS

Grateful acknowledgement is extended to editors of the following periodicals and anthologies in which poems in this volume originally appeared:

aag-aag!, Another Chicago Magazine, Asylum, The Bloomsbury Review, Bluefish, The Blue Ox Review, Calaban, Fireweed, Germination, The Greenfield Review, The Groundwater Review, Hubbub, Kayak, The Madison Review, The Mid-American Review, The Minnesota Review, Mississippi Mud, New Letters, NRG, Plainsong, Poetry East, Portland Today, The Staten Island Review, Stone Country, sub rosa, The Sun, Willow Springs.

"Ars Poetica" appeared in *Editor's Choice II* (Spirit That Moves Us Press, Jackson, NY) 1987
"The Lightning" appeared in *Atomic Ghost: Poets Respond to the Nuclear Age* (Coffee House Press, Minneapolis, MN) 1994
"Ninety" in *Wingbone: Poetry From Colorado* (Sudden Jungle, Colorado Springs, CO) 1986
"A Fall" in *Crossing The River: Poets of the Western United States* (Permanent Press, Sag Harbor, NY) 1987
"A Musk," and "Ars Poetica" in *Colingua* (NRG Press, Portland, OR) 1993
"Remember The Lamplight" in *Tracks in the Snow* (Mesilla Press, Golden, CO) 1989

Additionally, some of these poems appeared as part of the chapbook *In the Coiled Light* (NRG, 1985); those include "Ars Poetica," "A Fall," "Snow For A Thousand Miles," "The Lightning," "At The Construction Site," and "To The Golden Flower"
"A Fall" appeared as a *Talking Leaves* broadside

Copyright © 1994 by James Grabill
Design by Christopher Howell
Cover Art: "Osun Rainbow" by Betty LaDuke

Library of Congress Cataloging-in-Publication Data

Grabill, James, 1949–
    Poem rising out of the earth and standing up in someone / James Grabill,
       p. cm.
      ISBN 0-89924-087-9 : $19.95. — ISBN 0-89924-086-0 (pbk.) : $9.95
      I. Title.
PS3557.R115P63   1994
811'.54—dc20   94-10672
                                               CIP

Lynx House Press books are distributed by Small Press Distribution, 1814 San Pablo Avenue, Berkeley, CA 94702

Lynx House Press
Box 640
Amherst, MA 01002

and

9305 SE Salmon Ct.
Portland, OR 97216

Contents

I wish to extend special thanks to editors, teachers, and friends
Dan Raphael, George Kalamaras, John Bradley, Bill Tremblay,
Allan Cooper, Bill O'Connell, Phil Woods, Ray Gonzalez, Leiv
Kadmon, John and Lisa Zimmerman, Wendy Davis, James Kaady,
Wendell Carlile, Kid Gilbert, James Tipton, Barbara LaMorticella,
and Christopher Howell. This book is dedicated to these fine peo-
ple, to my companion Marilyn Burki, to my family, and to the
Family of Art.

"All music is what awakes from you when you are reminded
        by the instruments."

                                    —Walt Whitman

"The honey of heaven may or may not come,
        But that of earth both comes and goes at once."

                                    —Wallace Stevens

I.

THE WIDE MOMENT, LONG AFTERNOONS, SHORT WEEKS, LOST HOURS

ARS POETICA

The source unfolding bodily rhythm, impulse, local current
and grain, dreamtime sightings beneath workings,
the feel of a pattern, its content a species,
                              pacing,
passion and calculus of stalks, burrowings and thermal
makeup, infrared history, dock labor, how this developed,
that we developed, how grace comes in, that vision
transcends power, observes it, feels for it, sees around
it, to the planet holding it,
                              the webbings and links,
white shadows, crossings, sweltering magnetic extrapolation
edge that appears and disappears all over habits and speech
with northern lights, knowledge of an unknown working,
the wide moment, long afternoons, short weeks, lost hours,
the source unfolding
                      a future where buildings float,
angry drivers surrounded by red specks, blue light
back in night warehouses, the Blue Pearl that Muktananda
meditated on, became, observed, held bodily, working,
the blank of metals, smack of hammer, slide of sunlight,
smack on flesh curve, fields of Bach plants, fields
of the incline,
                  to murky soundings from far off,
that are here in arcings, tiny curled hairs on the cloth,
the slippery tonguing, throbbing of the pod before opening,
mysterious centralia,
                      jays in the air, crows in each feathery
atom, herons of the crow breath, earthen breathing banks
of root brine with wiry fish in troughs of the sky passing
over knowing ledges, for the latent emissary, the poem
rising out of the earth and standing up in someone,
fathers who give another birth, mother who gives an earlier
bearing, birth where it is summer
                          and we dwell, the cows
in each stone, moth in the shade of a short pencil,
the crushed possum where cars have been, concrete
with its ear to the core, flash of Brasilia at night

driving into Portland,
                    what lets us have the space,
that silver coins overcome their need, that the lines
of force in an interval near the conveyor belt
are syllables in the word Dakota, how the bending trees
bend not in space but time, and we continue
through one another.

THE LIGHTNING

> "It is the time's discipline to think
> of the death of all living, and yet live."
> —Wendell Berry

Like you, I have looked off the cliff
of life-forms and have seen ants on the rock,
and I have heard locusts in the harvested trees.
I have stood like a grave against war,
the months swinging on a hinge of exchange
in such a universe that lets us go.
                                I look up
from the sidewalk: massive nuclear blast lightning
everywhere—lightning everywhere!
Then there are buildings as before,
neighborhoods, people and animals, in this moment
we are alive, breathing in such a universe development
that machinery grows and locks into fuel warfare
of basements to golden-winged Christ heavens
we were promised for after the shift of truck gears
slamming shut to where we will live in the castles
of perfection, with the undead families,
and the undead beings of all time flashing
as one?, in a cathedral of the rising sun
and setting sun at once?, breathing eternity
into the tiniest plasm or twinge near where worms slip
their lost train of where the void stops twisting
and excreting lubrication,
                          as only the supreme
maker could fit it into an individual bird
or dog energy, not only a species, but an individual
then another individual and another. And what happens
when a person we live beside falls off the earth?
I look up, toward the shipyards. It is a split
second, atomic war, life as we see it, atomic war,
life as we see it, atomic war, life as we see it.

NUCLEAR SAYINGS

The horse of fire
roars in the leaves.

Moonlight is crystal slicing between blades
of grass to the bulging roots of molecules.
Worms of the moonlight loosen the air.

The bonds that do not exist
are severed completely.

The hands of the rich earth destroy the rain.
The lovely face of the animal
continues to pass through our houses.

The candle flame is a forest.
I look away and it is there.

TOMATO SEASON

The scent of tomatoes and spices
used for ketchup fills the air
in the small Ohio town.
Many fields of tomatoes
have ripened at the same time.
At dusk, workers are still
in the fields. Adults and children.
Full baskets sit at the end of some rows.

I don't know what to do for a living.
Driving around, I pass the factory
and see trucks still delivering tomatoes
at midnight. As they wait in line,
a few of the men sleep in their cabs.

Suddenly the forklifts unload them.
The forklifts whirl around, on a dime,
like helicopters over an Asian village,
beneath the heavy spotlights
that flood the parking lot,
as if it takes place underwater.

Beside one of the trucks,
three men talk together
in very loud Spanish.
Inside the factory, women
who migrated with them
a couple thousand miles
sit along a conveyor belt,
with a strength
you can feel across town.

I love the scent in the air,
from tomato vats, deep in the summer.
I drive past the factory again.
A man is dressed entirely in white,
with a white hard hat. He is a foreman,

sitting alone on the steps,
the father of someone I know.
He looks tired of being responsible.

A forklift whines, turning
to face another truck.
The worker pushes the steel forks
beneath a crate, lifts it and wheels
around in one motion toward the conveyor.
I see his face.
He looks angry
and full of power.

DUST FALLING IN SHAFTS OF LIGHT

I sweep along the black ridges
of floor mats. The elevator responds.
People have been all over this building,
like the thread of some kind of machine bolt.
Everywhere there are tide pools of sense,
distractions, magazines showing someone's legs,
business mud in drains, energy bruises on walls
and tables, northern lights on the mirrors.
I push the yellow plug of the vacuum
into the socket and hear the roar.
The overhead lights cast almost no shadow.
It's easy to forget who made this building.
Black combs are found in the parking lot.
The water in the glass on the table
is breathing.
                    I try to look straight;
dust of a high velocity shades us.
In the morning, sunlight falls in shafts,
between the buildings, to where another light
swarms like oil on water, and other streets,
inhabited by the models, or taken over
by huge silver buses, huge avenues, dazzling
signs, mother pulling children along green
storefronts, and now the night, breathing
in its sitars and its derricks, where stars
break open, deep in space, giving it form,
in the books of matches, or the lion's grass,
or the hammer's boy, or the cup's man,
or the medicine's starlight.
It is all disguised, as people,
as our hair and luminous skin,
and as rocks that come up to us
when we sleep, the night showing,
in the stallion's mane.

LATE IN THE AFTERNOON THESE QUESTIONS APPEAR

When we call out in our sleep, do the animals we used to be listen and speak to one another in their night, the hour of night, opened by streaming arcs of seeing an ancient planet has on the earth, or our ancestors have on us?

Will we die in a flash of human eternity, when what has been lost is pulled back up through chromosomal jazz or the Beethoven, the conveyors of Denver rumbling forward into gravity, plowing through plants of the only hour that has ever been on the earth?

Is there freedom in that hour, that silence of the solar system embodied as trees and basalt and the nine kinds of light? Is there freedom we can work toward? Is that freedom anything more than assertion? Is assertion another form of grace? Is grace anything more than following a pattern, animals given thought and forethought, and is the animal anything more than the result of that thought, the result of the earth's forethought? Does grace stand behind the pain and pleasure, with parts that fit together as if they were made for one another?

SNOW FOR A THOUSAND MILES

After a night on the line,
after many nights, now we can sit
together through these miles,
in a single hour that does not stop,
and what has been happening
is a snow over what I can see here,
Colorado moving in its ocean
at the foot of crystal slopes,
and we are still underground in that room,
Victoria dancing in ultraviolet.
Snow, before the end of October,
in our talk at the end, swirls up
out of the ground to where new snow
is falling. We talk through the miles,
the bristling, roiling electric web
woven tonight, woven this morning
and this long afternoon.

       The snow has spun itself
around each spinal column, around thick
cords of sunlight, down here in the night
of Saturn's Day, the drift of porch lights
over numinous pavement, the ocean slowly
receding, power that moves back down
into us, in this single time, this
earthen snow when we come here, thinking
toward one another, breathing the same air
and feeling the earth of our bodies
is not different from the earth of an owl
or magpie, and her cool slip against his chest
going open, alive in each grain of sight,
always a new street, always new houses
the old ones have left behind, as themselves.
It is more than anything we can hold,
that we appear here, to one another.

MEETING AN OLD WOMAN ON A DIRT PATH

I.

There is some blood
in the ocean. An old world
woman stands in the path.
She says, "Some are dead.
Some are gone. All is
here now."
                She says,
"But hunger is hungry.
It forgets it is the brain.
It forgets it is blood
to be planted. The judge
does not eat because of the poor,
and what is the same wants to be
different, to be recognized,
to survive.
                It is the old city
filling up the city, old hallways
filling the hallways, the ancient
chairs, the carved doors
of chromosomes in pulsing light
of Gauguin. The empty bowls
are faces of old dogs."

II.

An old man walks up
with a meat-smeared newspaper.
His skeletal light
falls from our bones.
No, it is the old woman.
She is very old.
                    She says:
"Everything flies back
into the sun. Everything
is where we find it again.
This goes on, past
our senses, and the faces
of beings, through time, billions,
in no distance, we can't
see them...
                    At supper,
we will eat the sun of the cells
of wheat, and the sun
of the cauliflower cells,
and the sun of the fish."

LIGHTS

The full sun and full moon are one light.
The full sun and full moon are two lights.
The moon having risen in the day is a third.

A fourth is the moonlight over the leaves.
A fourth is the crimson sun over the waves.
The sound of the voice is a fifth sunlight.
It is sound carrying parallel moonlights.

In the afternoon the sky is clearly of twin powers.
The grass is rising in its blood flames.
The grass is rising through the sunlight.

HOWARD HUGHES SPIRITS HIMSELF STILL AS JEEPS ARE WRECKLESSLY DRIVEN ON TERRAINS SEEN ONLY IN DREAM

We travel to or from a work,
the fuels looking from us, the right wing
shoving off, holding, as the bird
of steel turns midair above the work camps,
moving from one midair continent to another,
as the workweek bends beneath.
                                          Now the barn bends
motionlessly with the bird. Cisterns
with their thoughts of a void want to graciously
call down their master. The neon outside
small cafes weaves a nest of street blocks.
Elk horns curl above the small discussions
of Kant by the expatriots. Basement stairs
riddle the dream of a government. The stairs go up
to the first level, which is the new basement.
The elevator floats through its rooms. The huge
bird circles.
                        There is a light of arrival,
that fills the streets and apartment of the good
dream. If a bird moves, it was given a place to go.
If wheels are flat, the care of elders is nearby.
If the cafe is dead, another wave will hit.
If the light is too even, poverty will grow
like vines in your stomach, pulling down,
from the others pulled down. If the light
is uneven, workers are pushing crates down the ramp
from the train car.
                      It is a light breathed upon
by a field of yellow-brown trees. It is stillness,
that allows us, that urges, from beneath the floating
light. An old person speaks down the hall into a number
of people. The bird rumbles above. There are voices
even in the dust that falls onto small branches
of the trees.

(for Chris and Carlos)

SPRING SAYINGS

A person makes enough
to exist on frequency.

The cherry blossoms
open from within
a solar system.

The present sees beyond
the past; the other
unknown contains the seen.

**

A whale is the plow of a hexagram.
A hexagram is the whale of a plow.
A wave from all corners is a whale.

From all corners,
the whale is a hexagram's plow.

THE FLOWING

Behind the scattered roads and houses
a river breathes, pouring freely
as a child's long hair over the pillow,
the weight in the moving water, the molten rock
in the earth's core, a pod of seeds exploding
all afternoon, in the milk light of afternoon,
voices over broadcast systems, voices of gravel
and static, voices of molten metals, polished
silver, and dark stone.
                      Hum of the tuning
fork, stars in their spiral pods, solar wind
of people's voices, the river breathing, wind
leaking in the alcove, humming Cherokee women,
old men humming octaves apart.
                          Earth
eats her young and old, over again, wind from the moon
holds the trees, an owl soaring above the infant's sleep,
clock dials whirl in the galaxies, a fresh bread,
a cut lumber surfing on the wave of thick milk
and skins. Intricate organs luminous in the temple
walls, dust in the air bringing incense of honey,
a white rain in front of us, asking, wanting this,
to bless us.
                A dark crib is knowledge, the moaning
engines, shrill turbine steel hair polishing the grip,
driftwood of bones in the sleeping body, blood-filled,
for stones are already awake. Nothing changes that.
Stones shaped like fish, eggs, faces, promises.
Knock them in two, but there they are. Explode
them from their atomic cores. They'll sleep
through it.
                Everything pouring, blood in the veins,
thick waves of coal, dissolving ages of men
and women, fiery black cosmos floating up each
fiery hair, crystal books, the fire inside water.
Rivers of animal bones pour with wood and leaves
beneath the floors, the wheat and hay climbing

their spines, fields of space between planets
and the space inside molecules, a protection
shaped by the grandmothers,
and the rings turning.

(for Leiv)

TO THE GOLDEN FLOWER

Snow gathers above the bed.
Then winter vanishes
as you take form.

The boat of this house drifts
beneath scattered cities.

On a faraway plain,
workers have steam boiling up
out of the earth around them.

The great sun slows down
at noon
in the power
of each bone.

**

When you put your hand on me,
skeletal power pulling skeletal
power, we were dolphins
in the night sea.

When you touched my chest,
the way was a red road.

SUDDENLY TONIGHT I AM LISTENING

Tonight the rain enters wood through the roots.
Tonight the light-bodies we become sit down in our bodies.
Tonight in their ocean, dolphins and sojourns and maples,
    listening.
Tonight the cinnamon and curry and milk that is asking.
Tonight as low rumblings, as water on dream streets,
    as rain walking in a man or woman leading us.
Tonight amber from oats and rustling harbors of wind,
    and clouds of more world about to form.
Tonight the bluejay back in her nest, and her nest
    in our bones through which the night sky passes.
Tonight a horse breathing behind us, luminous, vanishing,
    as in their mountain, feathers are speaking.
A bird's stratospheres in the centers of air know.
Fire flashes from old camps folded in the stones
    holding mind, trees planting the earth
    between stars as between cells.
Tonight the wood carries rains through the sky
    of its body, into leaves and mind.
As all words form again when any is said.

II.

AS DOLPHINS MATE

ABOVE CRACKLING OCEAN MOUNTAINS

A MUSK

A needle that separates mountain hours
from daybreak hours blooms in the spine
of a cicada, viscous ether from stoves
in 1620, splintery libraries I can meet you
big-boy crackling radar sawyers in the timber
and stamp, they says, purple,
                        and slant-purposed
known wholly by mica glimmering thousand beings
in a fly's wings back through the canyon,
flaming limbs of trees in our veins, pumping
and grounding out over wafts of sacred hubris,
bittered,
        or the hoyden blossom encircling
in skirts of peppery bulbous rootage, earthen
diggings, saxophonic sandstone engines locked
on a helix of leaves unfindling,
                gyro-phoring,
mornings radiant in high grasses we have thought
with animals, sudden bedrooms of cool amber
railway linkage up and down the state, highways
that pass through each minute,
                 so when man talking
walk down the streedt unna dem flaxy red pants,
a male with hormonous propensity will respond
to the female, as if indicative of his underworld,
long tuberous herbal beastings, for her arms,
her shoulders and breasts smooth, naked together
in the night,
        held together suspended arcing
sidings and uncoverings, transposed through body
into groans and see flaxy walkin legs down streedt
so fine that sync-papa rang dem chillun true, wedged
between Tuesday and Wednesday
                    that the sax gears up,
searching that coast and the way she moves,
that he plays against, as dolphins mate
above crackling ocean mountains.

BELT DRIVE

In deep Buffalo, in the steel mill by the river, Hans loads
the bales of steel scraps onto the immense moonly conveyor
in the midafternoon, on a Wednesday, as in other cities, feeling

crates of oranges, shoes, lotion, or bundles of brochures
pulse, loaded on and sent out, through midafternoon tunnels,
shuddering through reptilian screes of machines, guyed whines

from ultraviolet grindings, baseline dusts scanned and pumped
out in time by passing horses as they speed through a boy's chest
to the 1953 hayride coming to stop at the door of his father's car.

What a fat! Women straw and hugs, shadowed by the barn-stormed
moon of alfalfa-cheeked ice-age banjo-gunned steam-glass working
up from late evening turns, after the usual eclipse of sleep,

and them journeymen still acting their grammar schoolboat
long-distanced resilient foundry deep in molten Cleveland
to make a frame on the green board woofing back your answers

to the big writing up there cranked in front with cattle yarrowing
behind the rocks that had reeling light eaten and partaken
through sage of auric blossoming tundra, the China flaring matches

in passing cars on a way through wakes of uncles of the body.
Hans shifts and floats the steel rocking through that black shining
hole in the ground that farmers plowed and raked, the particles

snowing back around bent green gearing oblivic and skewed oxiting
landgrass station, flakes from clicking heels, pelvic filaments
from pearl-clustered hallway lickered and oily heat of the doors,

of the lockers themselves, flooring night lapse of conscious
brakes thrown back steaming in blue-black leaflight, thighs
of oaken slowdance scout hikes, whittled back, into a hand,

the boy's knife still sleeping in its ore and raindrops.

Hans wires a bale and it slogs down onto the sweatbed steel-veined
conveyor in fall, as stewed tomatoes are swabbed out of the deep

kettle by the white-dressed woman at the changed moment something
could happen, like Kenny pull on Susan's pony belt jerkily
in grass of a moment that passes through each little body

as it waits in a line ready to eat something that will fill it
with peaches, that inks off the fool cows of the yellow paper
berrying some kinder to the children who sleep in the week,

who be inking off the fool microscope numbers moonlight made
when we went away. Then, ratcheting, the brakes are thrown,
deep in 1957 again, or in 1900—unthinkable for us, unborn,

the phosphorus tracers of a touch at the back of the pool
room hard hock radio amber of a grandfather's booming shadow
thrown into the room turning switchboard of august beams

when she touched his hair on the split diamond of an hour.
Nothing better, Hans forking the crates through, from a man-
pumping ox urge draining the love luck from those pennying

and brokered down wing to what or why root up to musky screens
of stars again those fathering fisheyed ocean waves striking
their fossil fire in hearts with grandma a girl then, waiting

lifetimes to look through your century in a curved glance,
the tiny porch lights towered over by your friend, on a July
evening, on her swing, hedge-mansioned, all hothouse odors

of earth. Then the belting point of night, when slabs of iron
run stacked and bands arc tightened in the mainstay swail-holler
down a ramp of engines and Saturday wheeling, onions, coolness

of heather, sunsetting through the backs of beetles, like spoken
hold of a hand becoming a hand, the rolling of an apple's light.
This hour, Hans working, all that is, how can it be incoming

itself and not sequoia-thickened by gulls watching or waves
when night fills in, whole ships of forest or ocean plunging
forward, through the star-filled galaxy of a seal's bark?

BIG PLANES

In this dust
The soul might migrate
Back to the heart
Though the silver wings
Fly in the snow clouds
And sound like controlled
Bombs when they land
At the edge of the city

A block away the wheels
Burn on the pavement
Someone else
Is afraid of
Is the reason
The cars change style
Each year

And a reason
The songs come back

The ferns become masts
Of the ships
Of the soil
Carrying our names
That have wandered off
And the splinters of lightning
That move in their veins
Are coming through
Our rooms tied
To the planets

And unformed worlds
That come from
What we do

ODE TO WENDELL'S LETTER

Your wild tales of awareness and congress totally assaulted my nervous system. After reading to the middle of page two, I noticed the hair on my head and my eyebrows had completely fallen off, and by the time I finished, I sensed added weight on my back, by the shoulder blades—I looked in the mirror which by now covered the entire ceiling and floor and saw 7-foot red and black wings with small portraits of women and men on each feather. Then I called up my friend George to tell him about how it feels to be standing between two mirrors, one above and one below, when I found that instead of words moths were passing between my lips, and each moth wore gold anklets with likenesses of those we might have loved jangling from the chain. Babies flew from one mirror to the other, and a huge dog's mouth opened and closed when I looked at the clock.

I decided to call a taxi, and the mirror filled with headlights, then astral figures, then solar systems in extreme expanses of the galaxy. I re-read your letter and white light was rushing up through the floor through the upper and lower mirrors, going both ways at once, mirrored back and forth, 2 rooms, 4 rooms, 6, 8, 12, 24, to infinity. When I ate brown beans, they turned into plums as they touched the tongue in my mouth which was vibrating with the vowels of your letter. I looked up into the mirror reflecting the mirror below, back and forth, and saw that each reflection carried me weeks older or younger, back and forth, until I could see, far into the mirror, to the baby and old man.

The phone rang. I buried it and could talk directly to friends I knew in sixth grade. I dug it up, and hooked it onto one of the highest cottonwoods in front of the house. There were fifteen phones ringing high in the branches, and when I turned around I was on stage in the Carriage Room. I apologized for being a man fully dressed in work clothes stained from the words in books I'm supposed to read but don't. But the audience hooted anyway, and I could see past the undulating ultraviolet lights that the patrons weren't men or women, but winged creatures with white and amber wings, and they were turned on by my red and black wings. I tried to explain about the letter and the mirrors. One of the creatures called me Mr. Drake in Symbionese-ice dialect, and as it moaned and clicked its message I could see teeth and pieces of ice falling out of its head in all directions. The room was beginning to be clouded over with all this white dust, and dunes blew across the floor in words other creatures groaned and croaked to one another.

I looked into a dune. The ultraviolet was heavy: the teeth radiated like in an X-ray machine, and I could see into them, to people in work areas, and cars driving over the Broadway Bridge. I looked into the clock, into the eyes of the clock; I was hearing its radios through its eyes, and they were telling me to dissolve into the wild, unthought universe—but I said, "hey, man, why don't you read the letter? Wendell does it, and besides that, for a clock you are very beautiful. Ever hear of the Carriage Room?" I said that, and the clock put her arm on my shoulders, ripped off the wings, snapped her fingers and the mirrors turned into a liquid that flew at once into an old ginger ale bottle I had been keeping because it was very old and had been found in an attic as if it had some wisdom. That wisdom was now clear. The room had returned. I thanked the clock, but she was so deeply returned to herself she said nothing.

THE TUXEDO

But what about the play we find ourselves acting out? In the third act, the Mother comes in, pregnant with the Father and Grandfather. The Baby says, "Mother, you look like a naval operation." The Mother responds, "Yes, Mr. Baby, your Father is in my belly and your Grandfather, too. The dark womb is full of planets and galaxies and Pintos and postal worms. The dark womb is everything you aren't. Go to sleep and try not to bother me for a month or two!" The Mother shuts the bathroom door. The Baby has a drink or two. Wonders about calling up Uncle Bob. End of the third act.

"What about the trip through the mountains?" someone in Chicago asks a basketball player with *Chicago Miners* written on his jersey. He pulls off his leather boots, and out of the left boot, cactus flowers roar onto the wall. From his right boot, he delicately lifts a drum set. He gives the drums to the Baby. The Baby is not listening. The Baby has grown elk horns and huge eagle wings and is ready to leap off the brink of any human consciousness left in the play. End of the fourth act.

So now, back from Safeway, the Father enters. In his back pocket, his wallet is bulging. He pulls it out and it is a buffalo. He puts it back into his pocket. "Yep, Baby, your Mother is in Here." He pats his chest, where his heart is, and his hand falls in and goes all the way to his wallet. He pulls it out. Doing so, roughly and thoroughly, his whole skin is flipped inside out into the Mother. The Baby cries and the Mother eats him. Then she gives birth to him. Later, at about 8:30, the Baby and the Mother are talking. "Mother, am I not the Father?" says the Baby. The Mother looks, pulls on the Baby's navel. The Baby turns into a buffalo. End of the fifth quartet in C-minor.

Later that evening, Mother, Father, and Baby are walking down the street of ancient sorcerers. The Baby spits up and a house breaks into flames. A factory soars down from the night sky. It lands on a branch near the Mother. "Look, Father, is that not the tuxedo you wore when we were betrothed?" The tuxedo factory works its way down around the Father's body. "What tuxedo, Mother?" Just then, the street begins rumbling. It begins pouring like a river of concrete. Everything substantial has begun pouring through itself, in flux, and another world that is steady can be seen through the impermanence. The Mother and Father realize they are part of that other world. They feel they are rooted more deeply than 200-year-old cottonwoods. They open the steel doors and walk through the crystal air, then whirl in the spinning wooden root channels until they are spit up by the Baby onto the silver floor. The Baby is on the throne. The Baby looks down at them. "I knew you would come. I talked for hours with the pelicans." End of the sixth transversal.

The Baby, regally, delicately, walks down the stairs from the throne. The silver floors are brilliant. The Baby is three times the size of the Mother and Father. "And now, my little ones," the Baby speaks in Arapaho, "you will receive the initiation." The Baby claps his huge puffed hands. The Baby wails like a moose. There are three babies, five, ten! They become sorcerers. Then magnificent cottonwoods from before Benjamin Franklin, from before Earl Butz. Flames are everywhere around the Mother and Father, but nothing is burning, nothing is solid. There is a sense of the earth flying through uncharted galaxies. End of the world, seemingly.

It wasn't the end of the world, though. It was just the Baby coughing. The Baby is in the crib. He looks up at the Mother and Father. The Father, by now, has great gray braids, and his face is carved like a totem beast. His gray beard is woven into dreadlocks. He is older than anyone could possibly be. And the Mother is also that old. Her gray hair flies out six feet in all directions. She looks like Donna Summer grown that old. Her face is also carved. Her voice sounds like the earth itself. And the Baby is also very old, older than almost anything. And when the Baby cries, everything vanishes, then reappears. And when the Mother talks, the Baby can see the earth's seasons, one after another, back and forth through time. And when the Father stands up, he looks like the night sky. End of the play.

"What happened to the Grandfather?" you might ask. "Wasn't there a Grandmother?" No, both were the same. And they were the Baby so many times it was impossible to count. They exist outside the play. They are on an Amtrak train to Chicago. They are going to pay their respects to the basketball player, whom they hope to trick into buying some land in Arizona. Arizona had been eaten years before, by a Broadway musical. That musical, then, boarded one of the spaceships and flew to the planet Marduk. That's why the Baby glows like steel sometimes, remembering the flight.

HOTEL MANAGEMENT

The perfection of comfort was Mr. Reams' dogfight. Because of this, he had employed Ms. Rhumanik and Charles and the Prammish twins who were born in St. Louis. No breakthroughs arrived with their trained migratory families. Reams had grown used to his new job as Hotel Manager.

Charles, on the other hand, was no side of beef. He was alert, in a field of crows and two red-tailed hawks circling as his impulses, a few luminous dragonflies, appearing, disappearing, and appearing from the grace of what could only be talked about as having brought into existence this marsh and the fast crows and the single heron breaking into its huge flight in the dusk.

Charles had always wanted to become a judge. He used to sleep with stones under his pillow and once he woke at midnight and could feel meteor showers. He had learned to hear trains deep in the regions, and he recognized those trains as something people far away were planning, and he realized he was separate from their purposes. He realized he was innocent and would therefore make an excellent decision, should wealthy men dressed in blue suits petition him.

Mr. Reams had reorganized the flow of juice between what he called the North Pole and its Lunar Equivalent. By that he meant he didn't want workers to join the Labor Union and he didn't endorse the Mother of Charles' monetary claim of sudden unemployment when Charles moved to the Hotel. So Reams worked 14 hours a day to show Charles what was called his Laboratory of Conscious Behavior. And no one asked what Charles thought when he heard the trains.

AT THE CONSTRUCTION SITE

> "If one is capable of seizing a poem, then all the poet
> would have to do, in its purest form, would be to say a sin-
> gle word, any word, and the cosmos would in that instant
> reveal itself to both poet and audience... Since we cannot
> operate at that level, and since we must fumble toward
> 'audience,' which is us too..."
>
> —James Tipton

The beasts of dreams look down into us
from the futuristic highway ledges,
with their velvet eyes dreaming through us.
Their wings feel like two days' growth
of somebody's beard.
                                  Like the crescent moon,
a neighbor enters and says, "I wear the snow
of womb juice and tiny army star like moth dust.
My hands are her old, liver-spotted hands."

Dylan Thomas enters and sings: "Here in this spring,
stars float along the void... They suffer the undead
water where the turtle nibbles... From the poles of skull
and toe the windy blood slides like a sea."

The agent slams the door. Demands to know
if the water root has been cleaned. His buckles
shine and his children shout from the Chris-Craft
he parked in the backyard waiting for the appropriate
mud slides. We suggest not getting his hopes up.

Q. Who is moving the suitcoats?
A. What is motion?
Q. Where is Lew?
A. Be Here Now.

The port of entry is the renegade solitude,
the circuit breaker of a thousand lips
and hundreds of babies pouring out

of the beached dolphin, washing into us
from inside each bone,
where the womb ocean
floats the mind.

MATERIAL FORM

This matter, texture, electric, behind each dot
of black ink the printing presses ride on,
down the slow slide of debris toward the 21st century
we know of as the tuning fork, the middle cross,
the abdomen hydrant, the screwdriver a man holds
outside Toledo,
                for when he turns, he changes
colors, with trees of each word, as they follow
the Mississippi of a person's voice in the backroom
taken sewing, into eastern scissoring continental drift
when seen from above the times collected into their coal
mines, and when seen down into a stamen a house reports
as its understanding of news, that a whale sings
as its dirge for the dead, that a wheat plant
walks back into town, the coughs before gym class
in the afternoon, on a Wednesday, before school
                          lets
its dragonflies of inspired mathematics in for the outlet
pouring its gloves of spiced months like a waterfall
from inside whatever takes form, so that a light
is pouring out, or showing itself, a center of light
flowing layers of earth, settling down into itself,
continents sliding in light, down, over the grief
of the ones, and over astonishment, the sturdy trunks
and arms and limbs,
                into flying and pushing through
ground to another element of ground, electrically jacked,
geared up without machinery, the tiny hives where actions
displace parts of the moving universe, where hair discolors
the amber halos of stars, where whales know their suffering
will enwrap a company from within, where plants know
that the living bearing is cyclic, transpiring, at balance
for unborn space, where people go, or cattle of weight
a thing carries into bowings, tuned in carved witchdoctor
periods, scrolled through the heavings
                      of the century
before this, that has been coming and coming

with its trolls that are geared, clocked, coughing
with moves, with combust, hieroglyphic—they say something
to a navigator, the totem beasts not in caves
as much as in dog faces and birds, and in faces
on trees, faces of breath before it forms in the summer
months that a person's shadow swings up before it,
that someone's dock of a personage or plant throws out
before it,
      and knowing we are one with the purpose
earth has chosen, we bring to it a bearing, a figure
of space that has been planted and picked up, saying
down an altar conveyor toward the wind signings, boot scent,
the heat truncated and root-felt, in plentiful wheatfield
or breaking wave of light in the sockets and helix
forming as what they will, and as we get ready.

5:30 TWILIGHT

There are locomotives
Of higher concerns
Flooded by the green spotlights
By the footsteps
Learning to swallow
The hammer full of the water
Or presence of a grandma
Who left her body in the 1960s

Hot lanterns over the fields
Of tall night grass
The strings of sitars
Sounding over the water
The ice with its decisions
The 1930s work projects
The rain and dark cattle

In the scent of skin
Young men unfolding papers
Seen through the amber window
In a painting of foothills
With the shining horns
Of a military band
Meat of the light's fog
Pumped up into the air
The twilight cadillac
Gliding through arcs
Of river light
And wingspans
Stained from the yeast
And sour breezes

CARD GAME

Partly on waves and partly on solid things, the cards that are half thought and half game fall. Each person in the game picks up his or her hand, and the part of them not in the game, the part in the waves, is watching, surging.

The solid wood of the table floats on the years, the way stars let go into the trees that stand. Sun gives some light to the whole wheat bread, and holding gives to the spiders and dust, already part of the plants in their waves, already part of the air the cells in bodies are breathing.

The cards fall, and waves in the cove thicken. The cotton on our backs could hardly be there, but is, as the road of the waves moves but waits, as silence of trees in the room breaks like a candle, as herons fish by becoming the marsh plants, as jobs work us by making us need them.

No way I'm playing cards, the wood of the desk says to the way we feel it. No way I'm only what lets me stay here, the body says to the light that finds it glowing. No way any more than the green leaves are green from simply the rain, or the picture before the sight of things is where the light perches. Any more than health is the hair scent on the x-ray wards, or a light panel pushed on before a concert brings some massive new architecture!

III.

APPROACHING FORM

IN THE MOONLIGHT

I. *Under Construction*

The throw of a branch
or bending of a room,
waves that arms pick up

in their hair, or moving
down gently to squid parts
of a cell or the light body

a move makes, and our words
begin to sway, to form
and unform, as they throw

their branches of rooms
in houses we find we made
in a light from cottonwoods,

and what we see in the forest
when we breathe with our gills
are totems, rising under our weeks,

curving us into ourselves,
whose world waits to form
with each particle of light

or shaded being of dusk
that forms and soon
unforms, and then forms.

II. *The Experimenters*

We wanted to stand
on what was given
but already
it had changed.

The houses of moss
rose and fell
with the breathing
of the ground.

We wanted what was given
to love us
and steady us,
in the wind of mountains.

We wanted to stand
on each other.
Then we wanted
the solid roads.

We wanted the cattle
of ether to stay
in the field, but already
so many were missing.

III. *A Car on the Road*

Even if we had once been
all things, the Ford
shipped us warm past farms,

past shores of lights
the one shore fills, creates,
the car's luminous mineral dials

seen at night for a brief summer.
Even if that young body
carried now by its older body

still watches, learning dusk
in hollows, the buck-coated
mushrooms following the moon

out of the ground will wait
in oceanic Oregon moonlight.
Even as mint hydrous in yards

may be held by lodgepole roots,
oysters wavering deep in wheeling
bays of starlights, Latin drums

miles in the books, with miles
of changed current dolphins surge,
the earth-breathing cells

gendering skin pressing skin,
or the pulse landing heather
with newly-mown alfalfa

fields in the time-stop
of a clock now, the old Ford
drove through molten cores

of voices from nearby cities,
electric, cellular, carrying us
all night into this earth.

SOME LANGUAGE

What we say isn't living
in the same way
a horse runs over the hill,
and houses of the wind
are the way language warps
when it is used,
or how money can disappear
without warning,
the way someone will come
into someone else's life.

And other language
streaks in huge sheets
of lightning over the city,
when the mother talked
suddenly from the depths
of her social self
to her child one morning,
and the child realized
he didn't know her,
that she wasn't merely
part of his only story.

And we don't have a chance
to perceive with the eyes
of our grandmothers,
we don't simply move
from inside our bodies
to the hallways
of prairie grass,
where words before we speak
come back to us
in flakes of mica,
glittering, jewelled mica,
and the scent of ground,
the scent of damp ground,
where the plants grow,
that we will become.

A METAL VALVE

A metal valve of a machine
is also the workhours
of workers who dug the ore
out of a hill and families
of those workers and metal parts
truckers needed when they drove
the ore to the refinery
and the Chicago street
a welder drives down
and the hill he went to
when he was a boy.

Our houses float each minute
down a river into an ocean
of that minute, and we go
with them, and we cannot go.
A bird's song does not work
without a source of light,
and the leaves around it.
The ocean's forest of sound
breaks farther than we can
know, passing through us.

Of what is born, so much
is not contained!
A rock is entirely itself,
as it is a hill
and a finch's song,
and a man walking back
from the car.

IN THE UNSEEN

Snow covers and uncovers
everything we did.
It goes away, as it falls,
covering the veterans' footprints,
drifting over shoulders
and arms that are part
of the trees of daylight.

Behind this, old people sit
at a wooden table, with a bread
we can't see from where we are.
We might not know they have bread
or feel the beach one has dreamt of,
that is still near her, in the waves.

And behind the hours of sleep,
hours whose waves did not connect
live in ghost worlds
of cactus fields, and the couple
sharing nothing we can point out,
they love each other,
or what a woman from the foothills
said about the elk, twenty
of them around her house
one morning in late October.

And behind the houses
are the furnaces of a leaf,
and the touch she gives his arm
when he doesn't expect it,
or what she gives herself,
when he could never know.

NINETY

The earth wakes and dies down
in a word or swaying branch.
The crimson bird in an old spruce
stops me in my body of fire.

My grandmother sits in her chair
at Thanksgiving, unable to remember
her daughter's face. She is ninety.
Her words break off and repeat.
My mother strokes her mother's hair,
lightly for a minute, back in 1899.

Little we will say can draw her closer.
The earth bends over our lives.
A squirrel watches me walk past
like a field of drifting snow.
In the squirrel's tiny mouth
is a mahogany food from a tree
he found quietly, through the pulse
of blood in his body.

Honking, great diagonals of geese
rush over the trees by our houses.
They do not see us beneath them.
It is before we are born
when they land on the cold pond.

A QUICK SCAN

Waves of sunlight break on the beaches
of garage roofs, and the small engine lifts
and pumps down into the chassis of its mathematics.

The man in one dream lifts the small handheld CT-scan
to his skull and it passes through, to the core
part that develops in the 30 years of middle age,

earth-trunked trees, in a rooting back of the top
of the mind, and the wind passing over, with its suns,
wind around the galaxies, pumping them into place,

into blowing-up spheres, in their chassis of midnight.
Where a dragonfly turns, sunlight instantly forms,
and C-spine husks of corn, dense flowerings that penetrate

animal calls the body remembers, milk-voiced aortic
violet streaming at dusk, filaments of stone buildings
from an old world exhaling still, through the floors

and single walls as we speak, loosening the wood
in riverous sway, the first time now, for what careens
down diagonal re-entry atomic forestry, grandfathers

our bodies remember, mountain air in their speaking,
a deer stopped in the counter-breath of a girl running,
bluejays wiry and electric listening, down hotel weeks

through blond shadows around TV rooms where a grief
scatters, refusing objects, then falling in shadows of limbs
and nests, spreading down the angled mile of a fish's fin vein

seen as a road, through its world. Someone not sleeping
might be carried, deeply, by the touch of a body's others
in dream, by long guard-rails of bodies, streamlined,

cavernous, the hours of training that harden a steel pipe,

the chestnut scent in a friend's long hair, the dragonfly
darting ahead of daylight, his bonelit sapling in uncut

grasses, or blue meditative day cut with a face-flash of brown
Cherokee wings of a hawk over the trail, or the thickening
of people, back in the store, in the ocean of lights.

(for Dan)

THREE FOR THE INVISIBLE WORLD

I. Song for Novalis

He thinks of how she kissed
his chest, how she held him
and he held her. Tonight he feels
the aroused particles of night
around the neighboring houses,
and in the trees and grass.

Their waves carry the remaining
light softly back to its glowing
nests. In his apartment,
they pour through the light
like manes of horses.

They pulse and weave in swallows
through fields in tiniest atoms,
where light turns back in waves.
As black ground breathes,
night blossoms in yellow
dawn of animals' senses.

The particles of night take
his apartment into their stallions
and mares of blue-white stars,
where flames pass from those
ancient faces into his body
and burn there all night
on the blue lake
where we are born.

II. *Or*

In the universe, the North Pacific Coast is a scent of violet dust. But who's that far away?

The trees are empty, and full, and dance as someone filling of dance might see them, bending with those who move with them, and leaning away from tables with rulers that measure the bird feathers of a tiny particle.

In the snow covering what we meant to say, the dancer appears in the billion swirling flakes, the sun deep in clouds over the cattle roaming their hills in sunlight, prismatic, or steady, until at night we are given back to earth that always holds us, in the arms of the one silently sleeping with us.

III. *After a Jain Monk Prayer George Sent in a Letter*

> "Embrace the heart, embrace life.
> It is the only way."

Embrace the door that is opening.
And the tiny nails of forgiveness
    that go down with the ship.
Embrace the heron as he flies from the path
    and shows up downtown in the display.
Embrace the old people, the old trees,
    the libraries unable to walk.
And compounds where angry dogs do obedience
    because the sun came out or didn't.

Embrace the barber in his white linen shirt
    in the blue glow of the game.
Embrace the block his small shop is on
    for a few years.
And the terrifying emergency theater,
    hold it with blood in your arms;
    let it go with blood in our arms.
Embrace the mother, and the father,
    in a person you meet.
And the loud cars in their gases of Jupiter
    here on earth.

Embrace the window afraid to be water,
    and the fountain of cooled-down embouchures,
    and the trombone and clarinet abandoned
    by the side of the road.
Embrace the sides of things, the circle's
    and mall's sides, with red scaffolding.

And embrace the thugs of the maze, letting
    the barker, and babydoll, and ghost brother
    go on ahead, and the blurs we are.
Embrace guitars filling up with hundreds of horses.
And the slow release of the shore by the ocean.

And the permanent council of coyotes,
    and the sentences pouring out fossils.

We are threaded and let go by this holding.
The ocean breaks on its ocean shores.
Embrace the gardens never expected in the maze,
    or in the gray flake of chestnut bark.
Embrace the gardens of thunder, the vehicles
    not of our making, and thundering dusk.

Embrace the morning and the sun.
Embrace the ground, and its breath.
And the people you are with, through all space!
Embrace the fire's atoms, and the atoms
    of suns and midnight.
We are let go by their holding.

Embrace the person looking for a body.
Embrace the cat who woke up here on earth.
And the things that will not happen,
    embrace them with the unborn body.

Embrace the forest scent of the ailment,
    and its way to disturb us forever.
Embrace the enemy, and the money
    that squares things off.
Embrace the winter fires.

Do this by embracing the heart,
    embracing life.
It is the only way.

A FALL

Then I return to the world I know, the heron
as he pumps singly away from the marsh at dusk,
the mixes of neon outside taverns calling to souls,
the urging, unknowing, a hundred million suns
above the fall farmland, bread light of streets
after 10 p.m., the drafty buses speeding past
houses where people we will never see are home,
symphonies like ocean volumes going unheard
in the whale city, symphonies stretched in time,
the rock unhooking a story, western song
lost in struggle between man and woman, city
and natural decay of what has fallen.
                                                I return
to the forms of life as they power the neighborhoods,
growing on earth, bearing children. The meadows
of the tables converse with Bach apartment windows.
Hands of the workers move in a grace of light
that comes through tinted glass. The callings of herds
blanket the minute hand. The train shudders,
its memory of a thawing river, the avalanche
of a blouse.
                    I return the snakes of that car
to the host. I return the willful curtain of form
to the beating of the dog's heart. I return the red nails
to the tub of beans with her glance to the gaze of Ganesh
in the centuries of stone carving. I return
these lifetimes of smoke.
                      I turn back the covers
on the bed. The owl wakes beneath skirts of pine
needles. Behind the house, there is another cliff,
the columns of numbers, mansions of tides,
of understandings, where few go after dark, where
urging longs in the scent of earth, the foliage,
solar systems of unformed things, informed
elements, the planets seen between distant suns
above the neighborhood.
                          We need the earthen cities

that fly over the roof at night, fish moving
invisibly in waves of a hand, and after a rain
the massive golden leaves around a person's body,
turn of an apple edge beneath bending derricks
and tavern salts, abandon of each shape we took,
in light from the roots of ferns. We know
we will live in each other until we die.

SOME TRANSMUTATION OF DESIRE: THE BRIDGE ASKS

The bridge asks. The small garage asks. Say round things come back, like yellow light.

Say the milk knows why it is hungry. Say the sun's museum is living propagation in a falling rain. Say it was a time and it lives.

But what holds to the ground asks. And ocean talks like nobody in the sky. Say the center of the world center of the world. Doesn't it curve and empty you of your loneliness?

What is it one person needs? Space, a work room, another person? Let your desire out. Give your desire away.

To the sound of a voice.

To flowered skirts or thick forearms.

To moss-covered stone. Give your desire away. To the brown pelicans three feet over the waves. To the wild shore rocks in fog.

To the oranges and grasses.

FOREST

The lamp in the tree
is a bird, a flicker
or grosbeak, and light
pours from the cottonwood
into it, and from the bird

into the tree of its tiny sound,
being heard, and into the dark
gigantic trunk and branches.
Each point, where a bird waits,
turns down into an open place

where it roots, where a bird
catches fire with the trees
and stands in the weeks and months
of a seed falling, or a nest
hovering around what it will form.

The light in a person's hair
is the voice that a body
speaks when the person listens,
or the bones of a face
holding back, in their pitch,

the plants lifting into us,
the unformed trees, at each point,
where the earth begins to see
from them, when the earth
surely sees from them.

REMEMBER THE LAMPLIGHT

Forget the passing of an hour.
Remember the kernels sifted
   for weeks in the shadow
   of the tall buildings.

Forget the passing of a hand
   for the last time through the warm
   light of a workweek.
Remember the hour beginning
   at the end of the sea.

Think of the tomato plants formed
   in their fields, from cores
   of an hour, from starlight
   of labor and sunlight
   warped down in its pumping.
And the factory where tomatoes are driven
   by other countries down roads
   with names of great grandparents.

Remember the blue they talked
   was not exactly water
   in the moss and moving beaks
   between stalks and the dusty amber.
Forget the immense ice
   breaking in its river,
   in the nuclear thaw of business.

Remember clearly the old station,
   the magnificent clocks that walk
   slowly through the uncle's voice.
And wooden counters where numbers knew
   themselves and people were turned away.
Forget the sea with no faces.

Remember the car engines hovering
   behind the strike, the demands

in the palm of the drummer's hand
in the auditorium,
in the greenhouse effect of chords.
And the work about to be happening
    in the cells, the heat being lost
    as names of our people.

Forget the restless stillness
    of the canyons.
Remember the theory brings
    its heavy scent
    that holds quietly.

The dusty lamplight shows
    around us.
And caves float their petroglyphs
    gnostically behind
    the transactions.

WE KNOW CAPTURE OF THE INFINITE

We know capture
of the infinite,
a stone that defies

chance, bearing its emerald,
our breathing bodies,
unborn, then born in violet,

from under the ground,
the swoop of orbits, planets
holding us to unborn

reaches, and what we know,
we fly through each other,
back home. We fly

into each earth that was made
before we felt the trees
that held us in their bodies

of flowing sun. How little
we have been allowed to see!
The bone stars throw down

their grief into plants,
and as we move, we let
the parts work freely.

So now this is! Dolphin!
Human! We are nowhere
where the grass is stronger

than the ocean swelling
through herds we begin as,
and we are thrown back

into graves of lightning
a tree shows on the back
of a winged beetle.

THROUGH THE DOOR

Tonight I feel you in the wheat
of the paper, and in moonlight
of each solid color, bending

to see what it becomes,
the way we bend at work, lit
by the sun as it comes from earth.

When I walk beneath the trees to work,
I feel you part of the power
that lets me go, with part of dawn

asking from my cells, breathing
molecular wheat in the light,
circling down through the bread

on the old table, in the morning.
I want to be with you at dawn,
as engines pulse on ribs of twilight,

as shape slides through its numbers,
riverous, deep when morning
is open, ready for us. I am free,

when I feel you waking. When you walk
out the door, we kiss, and swirling
in my light is your light, and firs

still thick with the breathing night,
where our deep bodies stay rooted,
and wake themselves into the world.

4 A.M.

To walk through the still night
of the rooms
an hour after making love
and return wakeful
and passioned to the focus,
through states, the owl
we can feel not far
from here, hidden
in the dense clutter
of starlight and pine needles
and foothills or plains
of neighborhood sleep,
where neighbors appear
full-blooded, miles apart,
and on the ground
golden pinecones,
with the secret in them,
beneath huge trees
of the open sky.

To walk through our lives
in an hour of still night
is to fly with the snowy owl
near the barn under starlight,
blessed with a chance
to be here, our trees full
of the ocean, moonlight
an approaching whale's
light, allowed to form
here, tonight this
allowed, early
morning, the pivot
of snow and moons,
of moonlight
approaching form.

About The Author

James Grabill was born in Ohio and attended the College of Wooster, Bowling Green State University, and Colorado State University where he earned MA and MFA degrees. He has taught writing and literature at Colorado State, Clackamas Community College, and the Oregon Writers' Workshop. His books of poems include *One River, Clouds Blowing Away, To Other Beings,* and *In The Coiled Light.* He is also author of *Through The Green Fire: Personal Essays, Prose Poems, and Poems* (Holy Cow! Press, 1994). He now lives in Portland, Oregon, and is Coordinator of Summer Programs for the Oregon Writers' Workshop.

About The Cover Art

A painter, printmaker, and professor of art at Southern Oregon State College, Betty LaDuke is the author of *Companeras: Women, Art and Social Change in Latin America; Africa: Through the Eyes of Women Artists;* and *Women Artists: Multi-Cultural Visions.* In *Multi-Cultural Celebrations,* a book which reproduces Betty LaDuke's paintings of the past twenty years or so, Gloria Feman Orenstein discusses "Osun Rainbow": "When the Osun rainbow manifests, both celestial and terrestrial beings come out to observe the miracle of creation as the Great Mother goddess gives birth to the Earth (here symbolized by the turtle).... Her entire body is a vessel of transformation in which matter comes to life from light and is propelled into the world by the spirit guide, the light bird being, that encircles the Black Madonna's triple faces and merges with her rainbow of miracles."